The Mummers come a-calling on a Victorian Christmas Gathering of about 1840: Father Christmas is the Master of Ceremonies, followed by the Quack Doctor, the Turkish Knight, St. George, a female character & the Dragon.

"You may wonder what is the Mummers' Play, and what is its meaning.

This is what there was before there was Christmas.

The Winter Solstice and the Turn of the Year was then celebrated by a play of Ritual and Symbolism.

Here we have the fight between Summer (St. George) and Winter (The Black Knight). You shall see Summer killed by Winter and then Summer's rebirth by extraordinary means. And then you will see the death of Winter. This is the story of the seasons".

So run the opening lines of the North Curry Mummers' Play.

Whilst delivered with all sincerity the statement that *"this is what there was before Christmas"* is something of a falsehood - for in fact the first recorded Mummers' Plays occurred as (relatively) recently as the 1750's and originated from printed scripts, not from some ancient folk rite. There is no evidence of a ritual midwinter play anywhere in Britain before this date.

The early printed scripts included few seasonal references and were more of a Combat Play which pitched a traditional national (or local) hero (originally St. George, but latterly King William or Wellington) against a traditional foe (initially the

i

The NORTH CURRY MUMMERS' PLAY

Turkish Knight or the Moor, with reference to the Crusades, and then variously Bold Slasher, The Royal Prussian King and eventually Bonaparte, amongst others).

RJE Tiddy, the greatest collector of Mummers' Plays, gave a synopsis of the action: "*The typical Mummers' Play opens with a naïve introduction in which one of the performers craves the spectators' indulgence, asks for room and promises a fine performance. When this is concluded the two protagonists appear, and after each has boasted of his valour they fall to fighting. In this one or the other is wounded or killed. A doctor is then summoned who vaunts his proficiency in medicine and proceeds to revive the fallen hero. Here the main business of the play ends. It is now the turn of minor characters to enter and provide irrelevant amusement of a simple sort. One of them collects money and the performance finishes with a song*". There is often a Devil character and a man-woman or Betty in the cast.

The play grew in popularity throughout Britain during the eighteenth century until it became the focus of Boxing Day begging traditions in many places: this being the one day on which tradesmen & servants could call upon the master and mistress in the manor house in the hope of a display of customary largesse in the form of a box of goodies. The Play became a convenient focus & centre piece for this custom - entertaining one and all, master & servants alike, on an extraordinary day of liberty. The Mummers did not perform out of a sense of pure altruism - for there are many references in the plays & associated songs to strong ale and slices of pie (and even gold) coming their way, and vague threats directed towards the master if these were not forthcoming.

The original printed chapbook texts of the play fell out of print and were eventually lost: the plays continuing in village communities by aural traditions. The participants were drawn from the local tradesmen & labourers, often the same people who participated in the Morris dancing team. The Morris was practised in the spring, ready for a few outings at the local fairs, the Mummers' Play revived just before Christmas for a tour of the village & local gentry. The play was popular throughout the country, with varying traditions developing: the sword dances in the north East, the combat & wooing play elsewhere, being played mostly around Christmas, with 'Pace-Egging' Plays taking place around Plough Monday (the beginning of January) with endless variations around these.

Each winter the play was revived by the players, with varying degrees of acuity: memories were tested & lines remembered and a little variation crept in, by degrees,

The MUMMERS' PLAY

as performed in

NORTH CURRY

SOMERSETSHIRE

This being a midwinter tale of the Battle
between
Saint George & the Black Knight,
the Death of St. George and his Miraculous Rebirth.

And this being
a Parable of the Seasons' Cycle
and
the Eternal Fight between Summer and Winter

as Compiled, Edited and Illustrated
from Traditional and Original sources
by
David Lawrence, Gent.

For Geoffrey Wilkie,
Morris Man, Mummer
Wit and Friend

Published by
DAVID LAWRENCE
Middle House
Windmill Hill
North Curry
Taunton
Somersetshire
TA3 6LY

All images, text & recorded material
(with the exception of the images in the introduction)
copyright David Lawrence 2007

All rights reserved.

Unauthorised copying, broadcasting, hiring or rental of
printed or recorded material is prohibited

Non profit Public Performance of this play is permitted,
free of copyright

www.fromthegreenwood.com

The NORTH CURRY MUMMERS' PLAY

The Mummers in a cartoon from the mid nineteenth century by Alfred Crowquill: from left to right we have the Fool, Father Christmas, the Turkish Knight, St George, Knockadoor, the Dragon & the Quack Doctor.

over the years, to the steps and the words. Thus it is that traditions develop and the plays grew to vary one from another: through the generations of faltering recollection and invention there arose a great number of parallel texts - similar in content and narrative but differing, sometimes totally, in the matter of the words. It was not until the early twentieth century that most of the surviving plays were collected & written down - a motley jumble that two centuries of 'Chinese whispers' had wrought on the original common scripts. Even though, in some cases, the characters, roles and lines had become hopelessly muddled from the original (and the narrative sometimes completely incomprehensible) the urge to mark the turn of the year with the traditional play, and one which most communities regarded as 'their own' remained strong. Indeed many were collected only after much patient persuasion & coaxing (and then sometimes not at all) as the participants regarded the play as private & personal to them & not for wider broadcast (unaware as they were, of course, of its more public origins). The plays (and simultaneously the Morris Dances) of the British Isles were collected by those who realised that the cohesion of village society and traditional ways were coming to an end: a process which began with enclosure, was hastened by the Industrial Revolution & the mechanisation of agrarian life and

The NORTH CURRY MUMMERS' PLAY

completed with the loss of the last traditional Mummers teams in the slaughter of the First World War.

The Mummers' Play, if seen today, is therefore a revival - the oldest being Marshfield, rewritten & revived in 1932 & Chipping Campden in 1934.

It is true that there is little evidence for a British midwinter ritual play before about 1750. Since I first wrote the North Curry play Ronald Hutton has published some thorough research (*Stations of the Sun*) in which he can convincingly date the first appearances of many supposed 'Ancient' British Traditions. The first Mummers' scripts were published somewhere between 1749 & 1769. It is possible that something may have pre-dated this, but by only a few years. Possibly some of the characters were drawn from *The Famous Historie of the Seaven Champions of Christendom* (1596, dramatised by John Kirke in 1638). It is also true that there are dramas earlier than this which contained combats, revivals of fallen heroes & devils, but before Tudor times there is really no record of a play with any convincing connections with a Mummers' Play - indeed there were few systematic midwinter celebrations before this, with the exception of the debauched midwinter Roman revels or Calens.

The pre Roman and Dark Age periods of these isles are not well chronicled, especially when it comes to the life of the common man - I cannot use this excuse, however tempting, to construct an argument that a crypto-Mummers' play existed in the dim & distant past and simply missed being recorded. *This*, therefore, is *not* what really existed before Christmas.

That *something* did exist long ago is not in doubt - but what exactly it was is unknown.

As evidence that midwinter ritual *did* occur one might consider the neolithic monuments at Stonehenge and New Grange as the strongest evidence. Their position & structure measure and mark the Winter Solstice with startling accuracy. Such constructions, requiring, as they did, epic investments of labour, organisation & resource could not have come about upon a whim. They must have served a need and a purpose and at some point one might suppose a ritual to mark the turn of the year did indeed exist. However it can be safely assumed that St. George & the Black Knight were not amongst the participants.

Sir James Frazer, in his epic work 'The Golden Bough', made extensive surveys of European midwinter Rituals, many of which do have striking parallels to the

The NORTH CURRY MUMMERS' PLAY

A midwinter play from Tyrol region of Austria at the end of the nineteenth century. There are some superficial parallels with the British Mummers play - familiar elements seem to be here: fighting heroes and a Death figure - but the lead role is not a national hero but a weary Adam and Sir James Frazer was wrong to conclude that a link existed between such European rituals and the British Mummers' Play.

Mummers' Play. In researching the traditions around the Sacrifice of the King to reawaken the Sun and of other Blood Sacrifices at the Solstice he supposed direct links with the Mummers Play & believed the British play was the relic of a continuous tradition. This cannot now be substantiated. The fact that the tradition is not as ancient as once thought does seem incredible and that such a clear metaphor for the seasons does not have roots in the murky past is surprising.

The term *Mummer* derives from the Old French *mommeur*, which itself comes from the Old Teutonic *mumme* (mask). There are several references, in medieval texts, to *mummers* midwinter revels in which a lot of drinking, tomfoolery & cross-dressing seems to have taken place. They originated in the Roman festival of Saturnalia & evidently got so out of hand that The Papal Council of 690-1 decreed that *"no man should be clothed with a woman's garment"*.

"The disguising and mummying that is used in Christmas tyme in the northern partes came out of the feastes of Pallas, that were done with visars and painted visages". (Hazlitt: Langley writing on Polydore Virgil).

The NORTH CURRY MUMMERS' PLAY

However the Mummers' Play of the 1790's had no relation to these original mummers' (other than perhaps having a cross-dressing female in the cast) but some association with earlier midwinter revellers may have led to the attachment of the term.

I first witnessed a confused, badly rehearsed and rather ungripping performance of a Mummers' Play in the early 1980's. Whilst being unmoved and slightly baffled by the narrative (or lack of it) it obviously made some impression. I was very taken by the emblematic roles given to traditional British heroes & villains, also that a traditional play of midwinter ritual and magic should be performed so close to the Winter Solstice.

It was only when I moved to rural Somerset in 1989 and joined the local Morris side (and thus had a willing band of potential cast members to draw upon) that I even considered producing a Play myself. Moving from a brightly lit city to a village without a single street light I was suddenly struck by the glory & sadness of Autumn, impenetrable gloom of Winter, the outrageous fecund explosion of growth in the Spring, and the mood changes of the season in between.

I considered the Mummers' Play a good canvas on which to express some of these thoughts and feelings. I made free use of available collected material and give thanks to the thorough & painstaking work of the collectors.

About half the script for the North Curry Play is drawn from traditional material, either directly or rephrased. There is extensive borrowing from the *Book of Common Prayer*, Shakespeare and Lewis Carroll. The rest is my invention.

I make no apology for the interchanging of roles, lines and actions: new tradition has to begin somewhere and nothing under the sun is ever, truly, new.

In emphasising the seasonal theme I had in mind the winters of those who came long before us. Nowadays we are all but immune from the dark and cold and precarious fear of winter: strawberries at Christmas; a thousand channels of gaudy entertainment and illumination at the touch of a switch now make Winter a time of inconvenience rather than one of fear and dread.

I considered the winter for villagers a thousand years ago or more: dark hovels, poor lighting, a tedious sparse diet and precarious health. The rain, the boredom and above all the mud.

Then indeed the Turn of the Year - the Winter Solstice - was awaited as a turning

The NORTH CURRY MUMMERS' PLAY

The Mummers in Marshfield, Gloucestershire on a snowy Boxing Day in the mid 1930's. They wear their traditional costumes fashioned from newspaper strips - in true Ritual tradition the wearing of heavy disguises masks the players' true identities from the public.

point of some importance. Who now sees meaning in the date of December 21st?

In constructing a new traditional play I have retained the main protagonists: St. George as the hero, The Moor as the villain, and The Doctor as the resurrectionist miracle-worker, but I have attached distinct roles to each: Summer, Winter and the *Deus ex machina* God respectively.

Maintaining the correct balance of humour has always been a matter of fine judgement: as a troupe we decided early on to avoid a panto ("oh yes he is, oh no he isn't") approach and to concentrate instead upon the message of death & rebirth.

Our play ends with a selection of walk on characters: Beezlebob is a comic devil character who speaks profound nonsense; Johnny Jack is the hard-pressed everyman who chronicles his woes as he rears his ever hungry family; Bold New Year observes that beyond the wreckage of Christmas the next year is likely to be just as much fun as the last and Old Father Time speaks of death, the end of all things and ends our mime.

I should address the possibly racially charged issue of *The Black Knight*. As the original *Enemy of England* he was known as the Moor and his being of a different race was not, necessarily, originally, considered contentious. This is clearly a more delicate matter in present times. In reviving the play I wanted to retain the original roles but I removed nearly all cultural references to the villain character & casting him rather as Winter gave the very obvious pun of his being known as *The Black Knight* (there are plenty of black nights around the time of the Winter Solstice).

The NORTH CURRY MUMMERS PLAY

The Moor can be regarded as an ancient historic foe, just as the Normans (in the Tales of Robin Hood) or the Vikings or the Romans. Modern racial references are not intended. In our play the actor has a blackened face, but this is drawn on in mask shape & is intended to be entirely symbolic of winter and of night.

I have gathered elements from various scripts & traditions to make a rounded play. This script is based on Cotswold texts collected mostly by RJE Tiddy and *The King* (Joy, Health, Love & Peace) song which closes the play is a traditional song from Pembrokeshire. For those who have seen the peformance: the stick fight between George & the Moor comes from the island of Guam and the sword dance with its dramatic star shaped *lock* is based on some longsword dance movements from the North East of England.

My thanks to Tiddy, and others, who spent the years before the Great War cycling around the Cotswolds coaxing the remaining fragments of plays from reluctant memories and writing them down. For making their work so freely available my deepest respect and gratitude.

Thank you to the people of North Curry who have supported us through rain and shine. Thanks also to the men of Taunton Deane Morris Men and of North Curry who have spent many a winters evening bringing a Mummers Play back to life. This play was first performed in North Curry, Somerset in 1990.

This introduction is intended to serve solely as a brief note on the historical & functional context of the Mummers play. I am not a scholar & this is written from my perspective & from my limited knowledge.

For further reading & reference:

Sir James Frazer: The Golden Bough (Macmillan, 1890·1923)

R.J.E. Tiddy: The Mummers Play (Oxford University Press, 1923)

Sir Edmund Chambers: The English Folk Play (Oxford University Press, 1933)

E.C. Cawte, A. Helm & N. Peacock: English Ritual Drama (The Folklore Society, 1967)

Alex Helm: The English Mummers Play (D.S. Brewer, 1980)

Ronald Hutton: The Stations of the Sun (Oxford University Press, 1997)

www.folkplay.info

The Mummers
will be performing
their Traditional play
in

Queen Square
NORTH CURRY

1.00 pm
BOXING DAY

The NORTH CURRY MUMMERS' PLAY

The Players
The Guiser
Saint George
Saint George's Mother
The Black Knight
Doctor Goode

Additional Players
Beezlebob
Devil Doubt
Bold New Year
Old Father Time

[Enter Beezlebob]

Beezlebob:

You may wonder what is the Mummer's play
And what is its meaning.

This is what there was before there was Christmas.
The Winter Solstice and the Turn of the Year was then
celebrated by a play of ritual and symbolism.

Here we have the fight between Summer (St. George) and
Winter (The Black Knight). You shall see Summer killed by
Winter and then Summer's rebirth by extraordinary means.
And then you will see the death of Winter.
This is the Story of the Seasons.

There is (supposedly) humour in this play but its true meaning
lies much deeper
For now we are in the midst of Winter.....

The place: a village green in England.
It is the morning of the Winter Solstice.
A clear and bitter night has given way to a misty dawn beneath a brilliant azure sky.
The crescent moon is still high in the Heavens. The Morning Star has gone.
The bushes and trees are dusted with a hoar frost.
Rooks and jackdaws squabble noisily in the stand of Chestnuts by the church

The NORTH CURRY MUMMERS' PLAY

and on a distant hill the Hunt can be seen in full pursuit of the Fox.

It is a rustic winter scene that seems a very long way from the green and warmth of Summer.

A few villagers have gathered around the deserted green as they have done at this time on this day as long as they can remember.

There is a shuffling and stamping of feet and a blowing on hands. Someone clears his throat.

Some incline their heads as there is heard the rhythmic beating of a drum.

A faint and mysterious melody can now be made out, coming from the direction of the local Inn.

And then around the corner, as the tune becomes clearer and more familiar, come a group of strangely garbed men: some bearing swords and clubs, some playing musical instruments. There is a knight with shield and helmet; an improbable looking female figure, with beard and coconut-breasts; a sinister looking character, all dressed in black with a black mask painted on his face; a comical Devil with whelk shells sewn onto a red hat to represent horns.

It is the Mummers come to perform their traditional play.

A figure in top hat and wearing a mask as a disguise, steps forward and addresses the hushed and attendant audience.

Guiser:
There can be no Green Winter -
All things have a Time and Place and Order.
So - Now that Winter's here again
Come around and gather in,
We wish your favour for to win.
This 'handsome' band is come today
To re-enact the famous play.

The NORTH CURRY MUMMERS' PLAY

A story now of Winter's Finest Hour,
Of Good's defeat, of Evil's evil Power.
But this triumph of Night
And this exile of Summer
Shall be put to right
By the hand of the Mummer.
So step on and see the Fight, the Death,
   the Victory.
And it's 'Room! Room! - A little space!' -
Let saint George come show his face !
Now in steps Saint George and his crew so bold
Their dreadful pageant to unfold.
And whether they'll stand
(or whether they'll fall)
They'll do their best to please you all!

[All sing]

And the cock he crew and the Win-ter drew his name u-pon the land. And all the leaves in the jol-ly jol-ly green-wood fell by God's al-migh-ty hand The frost, the snow, the win-ter's blow, the place be-side the fire, And with a rat-ta-ta-ta-tat, "Old Jack Frost's back", calls cock-y from the spire.

The NORTH CURRY MUMMERS' PLAY

And the cock he crew,
    and the Winter drew his name upon the land.
And all the leaves in the jolly, jolly greenwood fell
    by God's almighty hand.
The frost, the snow, the winter's glow,
    the place beside the fire.
And with a rat-a-tat-a-tat "Old Jack Frost's back",
    calls Cocky from the spire.

And Young Jack be green, Old Jack be brown
    now Jack is and and gone.
But in pretty spring all hearts will ring
    to see him dance again.
Here is Saint George, here is the Moor,
    here are five rascals more.
And with a sing-a-ling-a-ling let all the Mummers bring
    Glad Tidings to you all.

The knight steps forward.
He is St. George and represents Summer.
His outfit is glorious, but tattered -
He is a hero that has seen better days.

Saint George:

    In steps I - a brave and fearless knight:
    The Champion of Good, the Bearer of Light.
    To my great deeds there is no end
    When 'gainst dark and evil my will I bend.

    For I keep England safe, do I,
    (And that's a useful thing to know),
    Against great strife fight I,
    And I'll give you blow for blow.

The NORTH CURRY MUMMERS PLAY

Guiser:

    Welcome brave Saint George,
    And welcome.
    Tell me kind Sir:
    Travailled far to be here now?

Saint George:

    Aye, far and further ſtill,
    From Nurſery door to window ſill.
    Over the hillſ and far away,
    Thereſ not a dragon nor a giant
    Aſ iſ not afraid of me.

    For Ive been to all five cornerſ of the Globe
    From the Towerſ of Tartary
    To the Gateſ of Old Babalonio
    And back again.
    (And Im blimmin tired now).

[Rubs feet]

Guiser:

    And fought the ſerpent and the worm?

Saint George:

    Aye, the Lordſ of the Hill,
    The bold of heart, the ſtrong of will.
    Tyrantſ young and old.
    Giantſ big and bold.
    Nabob, Magog, Gog and all,
    Ive flaſhed them all and ſeen them fall.

    'Twaſ I who fought the fiery dragon,
    And brought it to Great Slaughter,
    And by thiſ deed didſt win the hand
    Of the Queen of Egyptſ daughter.

Guiser:

    And fought the Moor before?

Saint George:

    Aye, many and many a time more.
    He and I likeſ a nice ſetto or two, 'tiſ true.

The NORTH CURRY MUMMERS' PLAY

They look behind them to where the sinister Black Knight stands erect and immovable, hand upon the hilt of his sword.
The smile fades from George's boastful face.

A plump and bearded figure now steps forward, dressed in frumpy garb, hair net and stockings.
A little too much lipstick has been applied.
It is George's mother.

Saint George's Mother:
    And I am Saint George's loving mother,
    A force for good, as you'll discover.
    And what a happy scene do we three make
    This winter's day in 'Merrye Eynglande'-
    Oh, but now my blood runs cold
    As cold as any clay:
      He who enters next
        Can take your life & breath away!

And so steps forward the Coming Man - the star now in the ascendant -
The Black Knight
Winter personified.
All dressed in black with a blackened face he is darkness itself, *literally* a black night.

Black Knight:
  In steps I, black heart, black eye.
  I swear Saint George and good shall die.
  I, the Evil Knight from Evil Lands
  Do dark and death cast by my hand.

Saint George's Mother:
  Just as we were getting nice and cosy.
  Now our future don't seem too rosy.
  To see his guiless smile gives me a fright.
  Oh George defend us from all perils
  Of this knight.

The NORTH CURRY MUMMERS' PLAY

Saint George:
    Well in my time I've been a fighter,
    I'm not afraid to show this blighter.

Black Knight:
    Come, 'Brave George', you don't bother me,
    Surrender all and bend thy knee,
    Give up thy lands to Winter's might,
    And I'll let you off without a fight.

Saint George:
    Never shall you bother me,
    I'd rather die than see thee free.

Black Knight:
    Step up Saint George and meet thy fate,
    A blade of wicked steel shall split thy pate.

Saint George:
    Now, now, Black Knight, don't talk so hot,
    For your threats I give no jot,
    For True Defender of the Right be I,
    And I says old King Cold must die.

Saint George's Mother:
    Always scrapping - what a lad!
    Perhaps (with luck) he'll kill this cad.

The NORTH CURRY MUMMERS' PLAY

[But to her son she says as an aside]

Have a care my son -
Or this cuckoo shall have your nest.

Saint George:

Hold fast, mother dear, and hurry home,
And make the bed forwhere I lie,
For I fear no man,
And I fear not the man by whom I die.

Let him come, that ragged thief of precious time,
And bid farewell to the King,
For if my heart can bear the wounds of love,
My flesh shall bear the sin.

The sun, now clear and bright behind the church tower, glints on the steel of the Moor's sword as it is slowly and purposefully drawn from its scabbard.

Black Knight:

To arms, Saint George:
Now is the time to say goodbye.
Draw forth your sword and fight,

Saint George:

Draw forth your purse and pay.

Both:

Satisfaction I shall have before I quit today!

With bravery as yet unknown Saint George likewise now

The NORTH CURRY MUMMERS' PLAY

bares his weapon - in all its pock marked and rusted glory - a sword a season old, a trusted weapon upon which is written the cost of many battles and many victories.

It is now ready to stand against a foe (be he ever so mighty) as a trusted friend.

The Guiser steps forward.

Guiser:
So, know you now this fellow is very winter,
All before him die, or flee or falter.
Summer's revenge shall come with
Time and tide and token,
But not before this winter's siege is broken,
One slash, one blow,
On your marks: get ready, steady, go!

[They fight]

They fight.
The battle is noisy and gruesome, but brief.
For Saint George, after a wilful display of bravado and an ineffectual acrobatics, it quickly becomes evident that his resistance will not be epic.
Winter is in the ascendant.

Black Knight:
I'll chop you! I'll stop you!

Saint George:
I'll chip your chops and end your strops!

Black Knight:
I'll crack you! I'll smack you!

Saint George:
I'll chop your toes and make you drop!

Saint George's Mother:
I fear the poor lad's light has failed him,
Oh, Corblimey, Winter slays him.!

[Saint George falls]

Black Knight:
One and two and through and through,
My vorpal blade goes snicker snack!

The NORTH CURRY MUMMERS' PLAY

> Die Saint George all nice and good,
> Triumph Death and dark and black.

Saint George:
> Oh! Oh! I am dead - Oh!

[St. George dies]

Summer is slain.

He falls to the ground, twitches a moment and is still.

The Black Knight stands motionless but visibly shaken, now aware of the nature of his deed: for he has murdered a King - and such a murder has made *him* King.

The congregation regard with horror their fallen hero: they approach the corpse with reverent horror.

Saint George's Mother:
> Oh cruel man what hast thou done,
> Thou's wounded and slain mine only son.
> How can England now be saved
> When my poor son lies in his grave?

[The Guiser approaches the Mother licentiously and fondles him/her]

Guiser:
> Why there's ways and means good mother.

Saint George's Mother:
> But I'm too old to have another!
> Oh Saint George you must recover.
> Oh for a pill or magic potion
> To stir this carcass into motion.
>
> Is there a doctor to be found?

[then louder...]

> Is there a doctor to be found?

[...and yet louder]

> For a doctor I'll give a good ten pound!

The NORTH CURRY MUMMERS' PLAY

And indeed, from the depths of the crowd a doctor does appear.
But he is not the reassuring prospect he might be, for at a glance, it is clear that he is a fool, and a drunken fool at that.

[Enter Doctor Goode, hipflask & doctor's bag in hand]

Doctor Goode:
>In steps I, Doctor Goode:
>A doctor rare and true.
>Why all this weeping woman ?
>What can I do for you?

Oblivious of the crisis at hand the doctor follows the direction of the Mother's pointing finger, which is directed to ..... a motionless figure on the ground.... nay, a corpse!
The Doctor starts!
He reaches for his stethoscope, and after a brief examination in which a stilled heart has failed to beat he is able to reach his learned diagnosis:

Doctor Goode:
>Why this man is.....ill!
>But no matter what the problem is
>I'm sure to have a pill.
>For I've a little something up my sleeve,
>A balm to calm, a pill to ease
>The cholic heart, the urge to heave -
>Let me all your ails relieve!
>Come, come old girl - no need to grieve,
>Before Old Nick his soul does seize
>I'll prestidigitate a cure!
>Believe that I, Doctor Goode,
>Can cure his disease.

Saint George's Mother:
>His disease?
>His DISEASE?
>He is stabbed through the guts, good doctor!

The NORTH CURRY MUMMERS' PLAY

Doctor Goode:

    His disease or his decease
    I can cure with equal eace.
    Stabbed through the guts
    Is sure a great disaster -
    But in me bag I've many a magic plaster!

Saint George's Mother:

    Can you cure a broken heart?

Doctor Goode:

    Aye, and a broken head -
    I've the very stuff that's sure to raise the dead.

                   [Drunkenly raises hip flask]

Guiser: *[Sceptically]*

    And just what can you cure, good doctor ?

Doctor Goode:

    I can cure:
    The hipsy, the pipsy,
      the palsy and the gout,
    (If the Devil's in a man
      I'll be sure to fetch him out).
    The warble, the gorble
      the rumbling of the tubes,
    The itch, the stitch,
      the rotting of the pubes,
    The migraine, the peabrain,
      the stutters and commotions,
    Vox, pox, strangulion,
      and torpor of the motions,
    Not a one will stand the test
    Against my famous potions !

Guiser:

    Then to thy work, 'good' Doctor!

Doctor Goode:

    This man's state is very grave,
    And only the best physic can him save.

                  [The Doctor opens his bag]

The NORTH CURRY MUMMERS' PLAY

The Doctor rummages, elbow deep, in his bag in search of ......he wrestles an object from the jumble.

Doctor Goode:
    From my bag I take.......

A string of best chitterling sausages is held up for appreciation.
Titters of laughter cause the Doctor to look up and, realising his mistake with shock and embarrassment, he hastily pushes the writhing, bruised coils back into his bag. He regains his composure with great speed and returns to the performance:

Doctor Goode:
From my bag I take........

Again a furious struggle takes place; there seems that there might be something alive in the bag. At last the hand is withdrawn....

Doctor Goode:
From my bag I take.......

In it a choice piece of female underwear.
Now with some discomposure evident the garment is rammed back into the bag.
At last....

Doctor Goode:
From my bag I take a bottle of the 'Hickman Chapman' lotion, And from my hat a box of Tintantation pills.

The NORTH CURRY MUMMERS' PLAY

[Withdraws bottle of lotion from bag and box of pills from hat]

Guiser:

What's all this then?

Doctor Goode:

It's Allygumption Lotion!
(A hointiment of mine own connicoction!)

Guiser:

What's innit?

Doctor Goode:

Narwalgarwal,
Pikespike,
Oilboiltoilsoil,
Onionbunion,
Beebalm, bones and borage.....

Guiser:

Enough of this humbugg-ery!
Does it work?

Doctor Goode:

NALWAYS!
See - upon his tongue I place the pill,

[Places pill on tongue]

And upon his brow I spread the lotion,

[Spreads lotion on St George's brow]

Now stand back and
watch carefully for signs of motion.

[Withdraws and prays]

Oh merciful God,
Grant that the old Adam in this child
May be so buried .
That the new man may be raised up in him.....

With this solemn Prayer all bow and there is a moment of communion. The mood has changed from one of farce to profound seriousness: for here we are at the heart of the matter, the reason for this annual gathering.
For with this craving for a miracle, for the darkness to turn once again to light the motives are all are revealed - hide it in humour if you will - but this is serious.

The NORTH CURRY MUMMERS' PLAY

Unfortunately for all concerned, and despite his best efforts nothing happens.
Such is life.
The congregation, already sceptical, now begin to disperse with ill will and mutterings.
The Doctor is left with a frozen smile on his face and a corpse at his feet.
It is time to resort to extreme measures.
He delivers a kick to the leg of the supine hero

[Doctor kicks St. George's leg]

Doctor Goode:
    See - he moves one leg already!

[The Players rush to view St. George who remains motionless]
[Disillusioned they move away.]

But again St. George is motionless
The Doctor delivers a kick to the ribcage.

Doctor Goode:
    The pulse of life returns!

[Once more the Players rush to view St. George who remains obstinately motionless]
Disillusioned once more they move away.]

But alas the congregation is not to be fooled.
Our hero remains: dead.
It is time for the Doctor to resort to extraordinary means - a miracle is needed to change the course of things: a bit of Divine Intervention.
He looks around, furtively.
Then, in the hope that no one will notice, his hand moves slowly to his breast pocket.
He removes. and then slowly unfolds, a large £10 note.
This he brandishes and, with a flourish, bends over and wafts it underneath St. George's nose.
There is a distinct reaction.
One nostril twitches, then the other.
And bit by bit, little by little and by degrees the colour returns to the motionless scene.

The NORTH CURRY MUMMERS' PLAY

Fingers twitch, the limbs flex.
Blood flows through dry veins.
The Doctor moves the Cure to the left leg - and, as if on a string, - a fish on a line - he causes it to rise in a most miraculous fashion.

Black Knight:
    See - he moves one leg already !
    The pulse of life DOES return!

Then the right leg.
Then the nether regions - a definite reaction there!
And back to the head - it is raised - up, down, up.....
And with a surge St. George springs into life, lunging for the note (which with the deftness of common practice is swiftly and safely replaced by the Doctor in his pocket).
Summer is reborn.
St. George has returned.
Summer has returned.
He is alive that once was dead.

[St George rises]

Doctor Goode:
    There - I've done something to do him good!
    (I never doubted that I could!)

Guiser:
    Arise Saint George and play thy part -
    Thou art reborn with saintly heart!

[Guiser takes Garland from his head and crowns St. George]

Mother:
    Cruel Winter cut hard like the Reaper
    The old year lay withered and slain
    Like Barleycorn, who rose from the grave
    The New Year has risen again.

The NORTH CURRY MUMMERS' PLAY

Saint George:
>I should renounce the Devil and all His works,
>All the pomps and vanities of this wicked world -
>And its sinful lusts......
>But I shan't!
>I feel better for that rest
>A chap in Spring now at his best.
>Thanks old quack - hobliged I'm sure!
>Now I shall revenge upon the Moor!

Black Knight:
>It is I who now bends the knee,
>And with your leave I shall flee.
>But in a season, month or more
>Then once again you'll see the Moor!

Saint George's Mother:
>Oh Doctor, how can we ever repay you?

Doctor Goode:
>The ten pounds you promised is all I need.

Saint George's Mother:
>That's a lot for an old woman indeed.

Doctor Goode:
>What you say is very true.
>I'll settle for nine pounds ninety two!

Saint George's Mother:
>I'm a poor woman,
>(That's what you'll find!)
>You'll have to take the cash in kind!

[Advances on Doctor who has already crept away]

Guiser:
>So, brave people gathered round,
>Saint George is now made whole and sound.
>All know this - that Good's reborn,
>The hurt is mended and Evil's web is torn!
>
>But - if you don't believe what I say
>Come in you others to end our play.

The NORTH CURRY MUMMERS' PLAY

Enter Beelzebob]

Beezlebob:

In comes I, Old Beezlebob,
And in my hand I carry a clob,
In my hand a dripping pan-
Don't you think I'm a funny man?
For I've travelled all day
through the land
of night,

Down a long, short, narrow broad old way,
and been so far off I be here now.
I ate nothing til I was fully stuffed,
and starved in the land of plenty.
I have talked with a man who was fully dumb,
and sang for all the deaf.
I've been shown the way by the blind,
and took wise council from fools.
I have sheltered in a house with no walls,
from a clear sky with no stars.
From a jealous God who cared not
and a strong king all weak and wan.

The NORTH CURRY MUMMERS' PLAY

I humbly hope for the whole wide world,
and shall own all that's in my empty 'ead.

So I'll want no more
than a glass of bread and a bag of beer
To wish you a Merry Christmas
and a Happy New Year.
And now I've come I'll go away
but for that pleasure you'll have to pay!

[Advances on audience with collecting pot]

[Enter Johnny Jack]

Little Johnny Jack:

In steps I, Little Johnny Jack,
With all my family on my back,
And though they're all but very small
They eat a lot - and leave me with bugger all!

My pockets are bare, my hair's turning grey
I slave and toil through the night and day.
I've sold my hat, my coat and my breeches,
Yet they cling to me like sucking leeches.

I toil from dawn, I toil till dusk
My tattered wallet ever thinner
While the roof above holds back the rain
They devour my humble dinner.

So examine these children
And judge them fair
For our future stands
Before us there.

Why - Here's Sally, Jenny, Penny, Henny & Contrary Mary

[Gestures]

Large & tall, big & small

[Gestures]

Come children smile...smile.....smile at them all!

[Ad lib]

And say Hello !...

The NORTH CURRY MUMMERS' PLAY

[Ad lib]

Ah!
But to see a smile on each rosy face
A grin from 'ere to 'ere

[Indicates left to right of children]

My kin each year they grow apace
They spread both far & near.
And I always say that a child today's tomorrow's treasure -
But I'd rather have some gold in good measure.
So come my family and earn your keep -
Go out amongst them -
And make sure they dig deep!

[The children advance with collecting pots]

[Enter Bold New Year]

Bold New Year:

For now you've raised your Festive Glass
And every cracker's pulled.
Gifts unwonted and disliked -
Happy Christmas? Am I fooled?

The cheery bottle's running dry
And queasy as the vintage flies -
The wrapping ripped,
The turkey stripped,
The weight-watched waistline gone awry,
And broken toys in corners lie
For Santa's come and gone
(And Jolly Rudolph's left a gift
In it I trod this morn).

And as I gaze upon this scene forlorn
I'll make my New Year's wish:
For now steps I: Bold New Year -
Rehearsed and not yet play'd.
As Lazarus upon the stage
I'm seen to walk again.
Please come - come, with me, again
As this whirligig revolves:

The NORTH CURRY MUMMERS' PLAY

And let this discontent of winter
In glorious summer be resolved

The buds will burst
The leaves will fall
The players come and go.
So learn your lines
And play your role
Into next year we go

[Enter Old Father Time]

Old Father Time:

Whistle up the Devil - and his name it is......Mine!
For, as you can see I am Old Father Time -
And time it is to end our mime.

While all the world's asleep
Not a sage nor soul dare squeek nor peep as I pass by:
For when I walks I walks abroad,
And when I sits I sits at ease:
In every town a field to sleep,
In every home a chair.

This idiot-told tale signifies nothing
   if not to say
Now is the time to kill time
Before it is that time kills you!

..And for your time my thanks,
And with my thanks 'adieu'!

Guiser:

So, Let us celebrate this Christmas Time,
All good to all in all good rhyme.
The Circle's whole his New Year's dawn -
Farewell to all that's been and gone!

[All sing]

The NORTH CURRY MUMMERS' PLAY

Joy, Health, Love and Peace,
Be all here in this place.
By your leave we will sing
Concerning our King.

Our King is well dressed
In silks of the best.
In ribbons so rare
No King can compare.

We have travelled many miles
Over hedges and styles
In search of our King,
Unto you we bring.

Old Christmas is passed,
Twelfth Tide is the last.
And we bid you adieu,
Great joy to the new!

The NORTH CURRY MUMMERS' PLAY

During the song five of the players circle Saint George who holds six long swords.
They each draw a sword from the bundle and form into a 'set' of two rows of three.
The music then changes: appropriately enough it is a dancified version of the ancient tune 'Sumer is icumen in'.
They dance and the dancers go through various figures familiar to all Morris dances: half-gyps, hands around, heys and at length their dance is done.
It is time for the final figure.
The players bring their swords together to form a star shaped 'lock' (this always gets applause).
The Black Knight kneels and the lock is lowered around his neck.
The five remaining dance around - the swords are drawn and the Black Knight's head is lowered.
All dance in with a shout.
They bow and the play is ended.
It is done for another year.

The NORTH CURRY MUMMERS' PLAY

The Script:
> The script was written & adapted from a traditional midwinter play by David Lawrence
> The play was first performed in North Curry on Boxing Day 1990.

The Cast (as appearing on the photograph on the back cover):
> Back Row (left to right):
>> Doctor Goode: Dr. James Hickman
>> Old Father Time: John Mathias
>> St. George's Mother: Don Church
>> Bold New Year: Adam Bushell
>> Beezlebob: Stuart Lyddon
>> Little Johnny Jack: Mike Highfield
>
> Front Row (left to right):
>> The Black Knight: Jules Bushell
>> The Guiser: David Lawrence
>> St. George: Steve Dyer

The Recording:
> The Play was recorded at Soundbase Studios, Wellington
> March 2005 & March 2007 and other diverse places in between & since
> Produced by David Lawrence & Jules Bushell
> Recorded & Engineered by Jules Bushell
> The Narrator was Tony Wiggins

Musicians:
> Mike Highfield: penny whistle, pipe & tabour, bagpipes
> ... Mathias: recorder
> Jules Bushell: mandola
> David Lawrence: mandolin
> Adam Bushell: drum

> Man in the Brown Hat: Cliff Stapleton
> The Mummers' Carol: David Lawrence
> 'Cruel Winter' (Snow Falls): John Tams
> Joy, Health Love & Peace: Traditional
> Sumer is icumen in: Traditional, arranged David Lawrence
> Musical Notation by Mark Lawrence

THIS IS AS IT STANDS NOW. NEXT YEAR IT MAY BE DIFFERENT